TODAY'S SPORTS STARS

Paul Skenes
Baseball Star

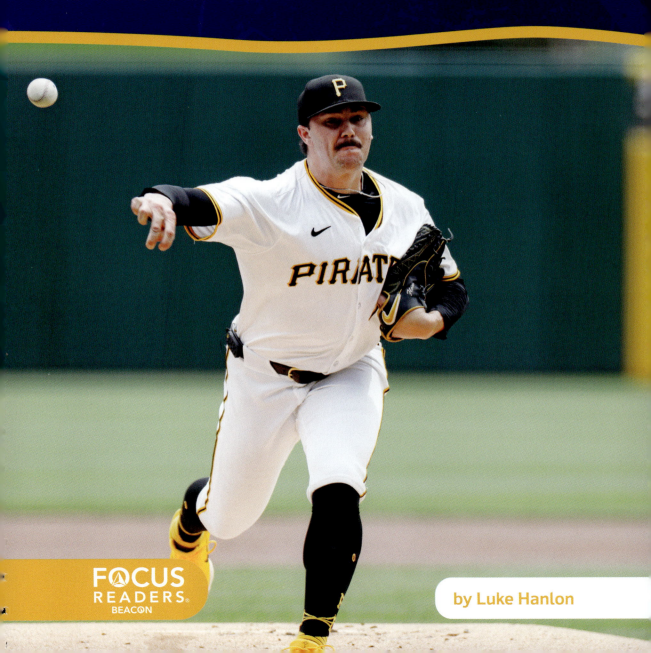

by Luke Hanlon

Focus Readers
BEACON

www.focusreaders.com

Copyright © 2026 by Focus Readers®, Mendota Heights, MN 55120. All rights reserved. No part of this book may be reproduced or utilized in any form or by any means without written permission from the publisher.

Focus Readers is distributed by North Star Editions:
sales@northstareditions.com | 888-417-0195

Produced for Focus Readers by Red Line Editorial.

Photographs ©: Joe Robbins/Icon Sportswire/AP Images, cover, 1; John Fisher/Getty Images Sport/Getty Images, 4, 6; Shutterstock Images, 8; Matthew Hinton/AP Images, 11; Stephen Spillman/AP Images, 13; Jonathan Mailhes/Cal Sport Media/ZUMA Press Wire/AP Images, 14, 29; Jonathan Mailhes/Cal Sport Media/AP Images, 17; Jay Biggerstaff/Getty Images Sport/Getty Images, 19; Justin Berl/Getty Images Sport/Getty Images, 20, 22; Dustin Satloff/Getty Images Sport/Getty Images, 25; Red Line Editorial, 27

Library of Congress Cataloging-in-Publication Data
Library of Congress Cataloging-in-Publication Data is available on the Library of Congress website.

ISBN
979-8-88998-596-9 (hardcover)
979-8-88998-622-5 (paperback)
979-8-88998-613-3 (ebook pdf)
979-8-88998-605-8 (hosted ebook)

Printed in the United States of America
Mankato, MN
082025

About the Author

Luke Hanlon is a sportswriter and editor based in Minneapolis. He's written dozens of nonfiction sports books for kids and spends a lot of his free time watching his favorite Minnesota sports teams.

Table of Contents

CHAPTER 1
Unhittable 5

CHAPTER 2
Military Roots 9

CHAPTER 3
College Champion 15

CHAPTER 4
MLB Star 21

At-a-Glance Map • 26

Focus Questions • 28

Glossary • 30

To Learn More • 31

Index • 32

CHAPTER 1

Unhittable

Paul Skenes was locked in. He threw two quick strikes. Next, he delivered a slider. The ball flew past the batter. It was Skenes's 11th strikeout of the game.

 Sliders are curving pitches that move faster than curveballs.

 The Pittsburgh Pirates faced the Milwaukee Brewers on July 11, 2024.

Skenes was shutting down the Milwaukee Brewers. The Pittsburgh Pirates **rookie** didn't allow a hit through six innings. Then, the Pirates scored to go up 1–0. In the bottom of the seventh inning, Skenes took the mound again.

The young pitcher kept dealing tough throws. He recorded three outs with six pitches. After that, Pittsburgh's manager took Skenes out of the game. The rookie didn't get a chance to finish his **no-hitter**. But his pitching locked down a win for the Pirates.

Did You Know?
In 2024, Skenes became the fifth rookie pitcher in Major League Baseball (MLB) history to start an All-Star Game.

CHAPTER 2

Military Roots

Paul Skenes was born on May 29, 2002. He grew up in Lake Forest, California. From a young age, Paul loved baseball. He wasn't interested in playing other sports.

 Lake Forest is a suburb of Los Angeles, California (pictured).

Paul went to El Toro High School. Several MLB stars had gone to school there. Paul hoped to be one, too. In high school, he played catcher and pitcher. He played at first and third base, too. And he crushed home runs as a hitter.

Baseball wasn't Paul's only passion. He also wanted to join the US military. Paul hoped to be a fighter jet pilot.

Many colleges **recruited** Paul to play baseball. But he already knew

 Skenes pitched in 18 games as a college freshman. He recorded 11 saves.

where he wanted to go. Paul chose the US Air Force Academy. There, he could combine his two interests.

Skenes completed basic training as a freshman. In spring, he starred on Air Force's baseball team.

Skenes would play catcher for most of the game. Then, he would move to the mound. He usually pitched as Air Force's **closer**.

In his second year, Skenes's teammates voted him team **captain**. He became a starting pitcher, too. Skenes kept practicing his fastball.

Did You Know?
Skenes had three uncles who served in the military. They inspired Skenes to join the US Air Force.

Skenes recorded 96 strikeouts during his second college season.

By then, his pitches topped out at a blazing 99 miles per hour (159 km/h). The speed threw hitters off guard. Soon, **scouts** noticed Skenes's skills on the mound.

CHAPTER 3

College Champion

After his sophomore year, Skenes made a difficult decision. He left the US Air Force Academy. He transferred to Louisiana State University (LSU).

Skenes threw 12 strikeouts in his first game with LSU. The Tigers won 10–0.

Skenes had started to think more seriously about becoming a professional baseball player. He hoped the tougher competition at LSU would prepare him for the pros.

Skenes put all his focus on pitching. His fastballs got even quicker. He could throw more than 100 miles per hour (161 km/h).

In 2023, the young pitcher led LSU to a great season. Skenes piled up strikeout after strikeout. He finished the season with 209

In 2023, Skenes led all college pitchers in strikeouts.

of them. That broke an LSU record for most strikeouts in a season. The Tigers cruised to the College World Series. There, Skenes faced his biggest challenge yet.

LSU played Wake Forest in the semifinals. Skenes was ready. As LSU's starting pitcher, he recorded eight shutout innings. The Tigers won 2–0. Four days later, LSU won the championship.

Skenes was the best pitching **prospect** in years. So, he decided

Did You Know?
Skenes received the Dick Howser Trophy in 2023. That award goes to the best player in college baseball.

Skenes was named the Most Outstanding Player of the 2023 College World Series.

to skip his senior season. The rising star entered the 2023 MLB **Draft**. The Pittsburgh Pirates had the top pick. They used it to draft Skenes.

CHAPTER 4
MLB Star

Paul Skenes quickly rose up through the minor leagues. By 2024, he was pitching for the Pirates' Triple A team. Triple A is the highest level before MLB.

 In 2023, Skenes moved up two minor league levels in only five games.

 In his first MLB start, Skenes threw 17 pitches of 100 miles per hour (161 km/h) or more.

Skenes started seven games at the Triple A level. Hitters could barely make contact against his pitches. So, the Pirates called him up to the big leagues.

Skenes made his MLB **debut** on May 11, 2024. The Pirates hosted the Chicago Cubs. More than 34,000 fans roared as Skenes took the mound. The rookie didn't let them down. He struck out the first batter he faced. Skenes finished the game with seven strikeouts. The Pirates won 10–9.

Skenes was even better in his second start. Facing the Cubs again, he struck out 11 batters. He didn't allow a hit in six innings.

Skenes took the majors by storm. He overpowered hitters with his fastball. And he fooled them with his slider. He finished the season with 170 strikeouts. That broke the Pirates' rookie record for strikeouts in a season.

Did You Know?
In 2024, Skenes donated $100 per strikeout. The money went toward US military veterans. His strikeouts led to $17,000 in donations.

▶ **In 2024, the Pirates went 15–8 in games that Skenes started.**

Skenes won the National League Rookie of the Year Award for the 2024 season. At 22, he was already one of the best pitchers in baseball. Pittsburgh fans couldn't wait to watch their star for years to come.

AT-A-GLANCE MAP

Paul Skenes

- Height: 6 feet, 6 inches (198 cm)
- Weight: 235 pounds (107 kg)
- Birth date: May 29, 2002
- Birthplace: Fullerton, California
- College: Air Force Academy (Colorado Springs, Colorado) (2020–2022); Louisiana State University (Baton Rouge, Louisiana) (2023)
- Minor league teams: Florida Complex League Pirates (2023); Bradenton Marauders (2023); Altoona Curve (2023); Indianapolis Indians (2024)
- MLB team: Pittsburgh Pirates (2024–)
- Major awards: NCAA national championship (2023); MLB All-Star (2024); NL Rookie of the Year (2024)

Focus Questions

Write your answers on a separate piece of paper.

1. Write a paragraph that explains the main ideas of Chapter 3.
2. Do you think Paul Skenes should have finished college? Why or why not?
3. When did Paul Skenes begin playing in the majors?
   - **A.** 2022
   - **B.** 2023
   - **C.** 2024
4. Why did Skenes want to play at LSU?
   - **A.** He didn't want to play baseball anymore.
   - **B.** The Air Force asked him to leave.
   - **C.** He wanted to pitch against better hitters.

5. What does **passion** mean in this book?

*Baseball wasn't Paul's only **passion**. He also wanted to join the US military. Paul hoped to be a fighter jet pilot.*

    A. a difficult job
    B. a strong interest
    C. a type of sport

6. What does **transferred** mean in this book?

*After his sophomore year, Skenes made a difficult decision. He left the US Air Force Academy. He **transferred** to Louisiana State University (LSU).*

    A. moved to a new school
    B. stopped playing a game
    C. flew a fighter jet

Answer key on page 32.

Glossary

captain
A team's leader.

closer
A pitcher who enters a game late to protect a small lead.

debut
First appearance.

draft
A system that allows teams to acquire new players coming into a league.

no-hitter
A game in which a pitcher does not allow any hits.

prospect
A player who is likely to be successful in the future.

recruited
Tried to persuade someone to attend a college, usually to play sports.

rookie
A professional athlete in his or her first year.

scouts
People whose jobs involve looking for talented young players.

To Learn More

BOOKS

Hanlon, Luke. *Pittsburgh Pirates All-Time Greats*. Press Box Books, 2024.

Lowe, Alexander. *G.O.A.T. Baseball Pitchers*. Lerner Publications, 2022.

Tischler, Joe. *Pittsburgh Pirates*. Creative Education, 2024.

NOTE TO EDUCATORS

Visit **www.focusreaders.com** to find lesson plans, activities, links, and other resources related to this title.

Index

A
All-Star Game, 7

C
Chicago Cubs, 23
College World Series, 17–18

D
Dick Howser Trophy, 18

E
El Toro High School, 10

F
fastballs, 12, 16, 24

L
Lake Forest, California, 9
Louisiana State University (LSU), 15–18

M
Milwaukee Brewers, 6
minor leagues, 21–22

P
Pittsburgh Pirates, 6–7, 19, 21–25

S
slider, 5, 24
strikeouts, 5, 16–17, 23–24

U
US Air Force Academy, 11–12, 15

W
Wake Forest, 18

Answer Key: 1. Answers will vary; 2. Answers will vary; 3. C; 4. C; 5. B; 6. A